The Ancient Parishes, Townships and Chapelries of Cheshire

by

F.I. DUNN
County and Diocesan Archivist

Cheshire Record Office and Chester Diocesan Record Office
© Cheshire County Council 1987.

Printed for the Cheshire Record Office
by Chelma Graphics, Print and Design
Chester

ISBN   0 906758 14 9

CONTENTS

ACKNOWLEDGEMENTS

The author's debt to the following is gratefully acknowledged.

Janet Ferguson of the Cheshire Record Office for assiduous checking of text, map and original sources. Pamela Holland of EDUTEC for the splendid draftmanship displayed in the maps and for even greater patience in coping with an atrocious first draft and endless revisions. To Jean Fortune of the Cheshire Record Office for performing an exactly parallel task with the text. To Eileen Simpson for initial checking of the lists. To Dr Alan Thacker of the *Victoria History of Cheshire* for much scholarly advice and stimulating discussion, and especially for proof-reading the booklet with an expert eye. The Victoria History is also thanked for providing the small base maps of the hundreds and the ancient diocese.

SCOPE AND NATURE OF THE WORK

For a long time there has been a need for an accurate map and list of Cheshire parishes and townships. Such information is essential for the historian, the genealogist and anyone having to do with the records of the county and the diocese. The task of compiling such a work is comparatively easy for the southern and eastern counties of Britain where parishes tend to contain only one or two townships. For the North West, however, the situation is infinitely more complicated as Dorothy Sylvester demonstrated in her article "Parish and Township in Cheshire And North-East Wales" *Journal of the Chester Archaeological Soc.* LIV 23-35 (1967). Indeed, Cheshire has some of the largest parishes in England in terms of number of townships, Prestbury for example having 38 at its largest discernible extent and Great Budworth 34. Understandably the distance of some of these outlying townships from the mother church gave rise to a continuing succession of dependent chapelries and chapels of ease.

It is therefore difficult, and to some degree unhelpful, to try to "freeze" the picture of the county at a particular stage. This map and booklet seeks to aid anyone working in a period from say 1200 to 1800. Neither map nor list takes any account of the revolutionary local government reforms, or of the great wave of new parochial districts and parishes of the nineteenth century. These are dealt with by Professor FA Youngs in volume II of his *Guide to the Administrative Units of England,* published by the Royal Historical Society in 1991. *VCH Ches.* II 102-240 has a list of the later civil parishes. Similarly, the origins of the most ancient parishes, and their link with early great estates, is beyond the scope of this work and is admirably dealt with by Dr Alan Thacker in *VCH Ches.* I 263ff.

The intervening six centuries are, however, complicated enough. A situation "where parishes were especially large and their numerous dependent chapels were of uncertain status and fluctuating existence" (*VCH Ches.* III 37) has defeated several writers. Samuel Lewis's *A Topographical Dictionary of England,* which purported to deal with parishes and townships, is a useful source for most places and had run to seven editions by 1849 . He makes a poor showing for Cheshire, however, and the entries are full of omissions and confusions. Dorothy Sylvester's list in *The Historical Atlas of Cheshire* (1958) was a noble pioneering effort, though numerous corrections have come to light since it was printed, and the small format of the Atlas rendered the map very difficult to use and limited its value.

The large number of detached parts of townships lying in other townships which do not necessarily respect parish or chapelry boundaries, tend to produce confusion worse confounded. For the precise location of these it is essential to use the tithe and O.S. maps. No doubt further research will enable additions and corrections to be made to the information given in the present booklet and some uncertainties to be cleared up.

It should be made absolutely clear that the lists do not constitute a comprehensive gazetteer of Cheshire place-names. For this the reader is referred to John Dodgson's monumental work, *The Place-Names of Cheshire,* which, with Ormerod and *The Victoria History* of the County, makes up the trio of most important and indispensable printed sources for anyone working on the history of Cheshire.

LIST OF PRINCIPAL SOURCES
AND ABBREVIATIONS USED

EDT   The invaluable series of maps and apportionments made for most parishes in accordance with the Tithe Act, 1836, 6 & 7 William IV c.71 s49. EDT refers to copies of maps in the Chester Diocesan Record Office and is followed by a number indicating the parish or township in question.

EDV 7/1   Replies by the clergy of the Diocese to articles of enquiry sent out in 1778 by Bishop Porteous preparatory to Visitation. The original returns are held in the Chester Diocesan Record Office. Later "articles" are also useful to consult eg EDV 7/2 (1789), EDV 7/3 (1804), EDV 7/4 (1811), EDV 7/6 (1821).

Gastrell   *Notitia Cestriensis or Historical Notices of the Diocese of Chester* by Francis Gastrell, Bishop of Chester (1714-1725). The original Ms is held in the Chester Diocesan Record Office ref. EDA 3/3 and was edited by F R Raines for the Chetham Society Vol. VIII, 1845, to which page numbers refer.

—   Annual Land Tax Assessments by Township 1780-1832, deposited with the Clerk of the Peace.

Cheshire Record Office
QDV 2

Leycester   "A Survey of All the Churches & Chappels in Cheshire. Carefully Collected in Every Hundred by it Selfe, togather with the Townes belonginge to every Parish, and the Mise thereof; By me Peter Leycester Anno Domini 1671".

Cheshire Record Office
Tabley Ms
DLT/ B /27 ff.37-73

A condensed version was printed by Sir Peter Leycester in his *Historical Antiquities ..... concerning Cheshire* (1673) 192 ff and reprinted Orm I 399 ff.

Orm   George Ormerod *The History of the County Palatine and City of Chester* 3 vol. 2nd Edn. revised and edited by T Helsby (1882).

O.S.   Ordnance Survey. For an accurate depiction of boundaries of townships it is essential to use the early 1 inch scale O.S. Cheshire TITHE INDEX EDITION issued in the 1870s and 1880s. The 1st Edn. of the 6 inch O.S. survey (1881-2) is also invaluable for the identification of detached portions of townships.

P N C   J. McN. Dodgson *The Place-Names of Cheshire* 1970- (5 parts to date). English Place-Name Society Vols. 44,45,46,47,48,54.

—   *Population. Comparative Account of the Population of Great Britain in the years 1801, 1811, 1821 and 1831 etc.* Ordered by the House of Commons to be printed 19 Oct 1831. (Cheshire portion pp. 38-48).

VCH Ches   *Victoria History of the County of Chester* 1979- (3 vols to date).

1740 map   *A Map of the Diocese of Chester divided into Deaneries* by T H (Probably Thomas Hutchinson) c1740. This map endeavours to differentiate the status of parish churches, parochial chapels, chapels of ease etc, though no parish or township boundaries are shown. The dating is approximate and is deduced from the map's dedication to Samuel [Peploe] Bishop of Chester (1726-1752). A later (apparently early 19th cent.) printed table is generally found in company with the map.

HUNDREDS

At the Conquest the counties or shires were already subdivided, for administrative purposes, into districts called, in most places, hundreds. The medieval hundreds of Cheshire were, if we discount the two lost to Wales, broadly similar to those recorded in the Domesday Survey (See *VCH Ches* I) but reduced in number by amalgamation to 7, and differently named. The dates of these changes have still not been adequately researched. Leycester conjectured them not to be older than the reign of Edward III (1327-1377) though all the post Domesday names are in use by the time of the extant County Court and Eyre Rolls of Chester 1259/60. Moreover John Dodgson has found Macclesfield Hundred so referred to as early as 1242 and Eddisbury in the late 12th century. For a general discussion of hundreds and their use as administrative units see Helen M Jewell *English Local Administration In The Middle Ages* (1972) 47-51.

In the list of townships they are abbreviated thus:

Broxton	BR
Bucklow	BU
Eddisbury	ED
Macclesfield	MA
Nantwich	NA
Northwich	NO
Wirral	WI

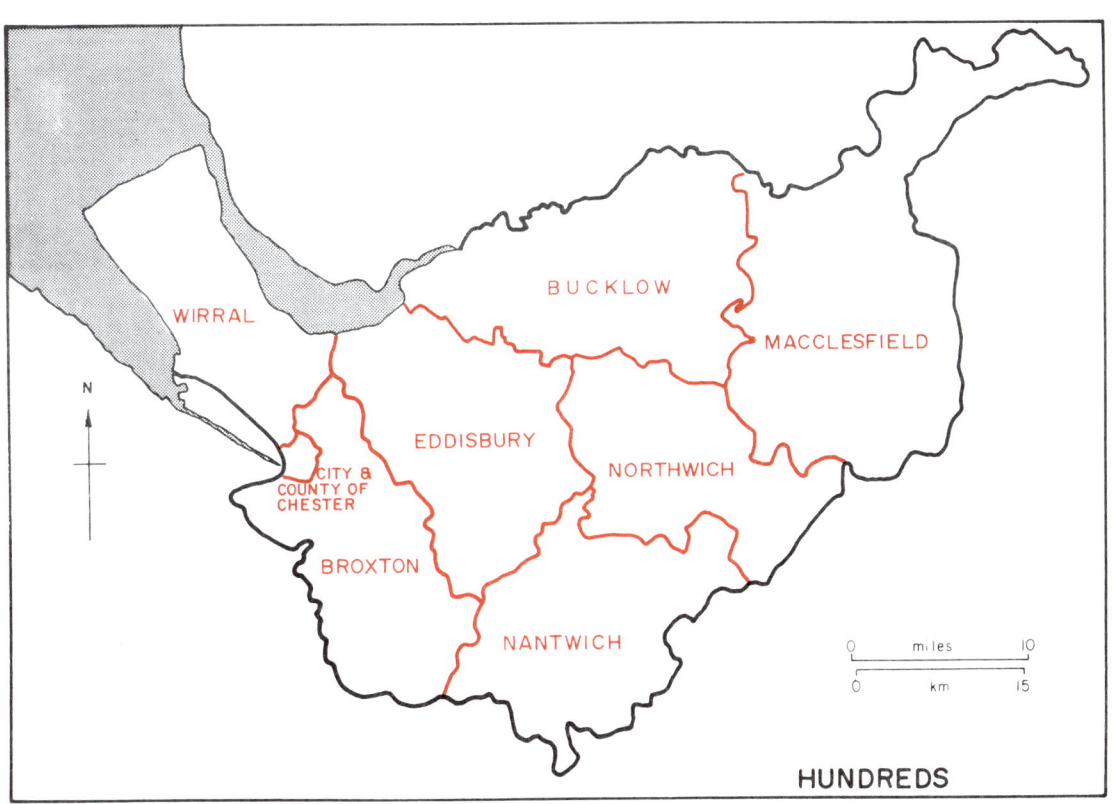

HUNDREDS

THE DIOCESE AND THE DEANERIES

From at least a century before the Conquest until 1541, the boundaries of the diocese of Coventry and Lichfield in which Cheshire lay did not change.

Chester was the principal of the five archdeaconries of the diocese from the 12th century and certainly by the beginning of the 14th century the archdeacon of Chester had acquired a measure of independence from the Bishop (*VCH Ches* III 8-9).

The new diocese of Chester created under Henry VIII in 1541 included, in addition to Cheshire, and Lancashire, parts of Westmorland, Cumberland, Yorkshire and Wales. The reforms of the 19th century are shown on the map and were eventually to lead to a diocese almost exactly coterminous with the ancient county of Chester.

The jurisdiction of the rural deans is also of some interest in the medieval period, though merging with that of the archdeacons in the 17th century (*VCH Ches* III 10-11 and 30). The Chester deaneries were certainly established by 1224 and were not changed, so far as Cheshire is concerned, until Bishop Jacobson's reforms of 1880.

In the list of townships they are abbreviated thus:

Chester	CS
Frodsham	FR
Macclesfield	MC
Malpas	ML
Middlewich	MD
Nantwich	NN
Wirral	WR

THE ANCIENT DIOCESE OF CHESTER
WITH ITS DEANERIES

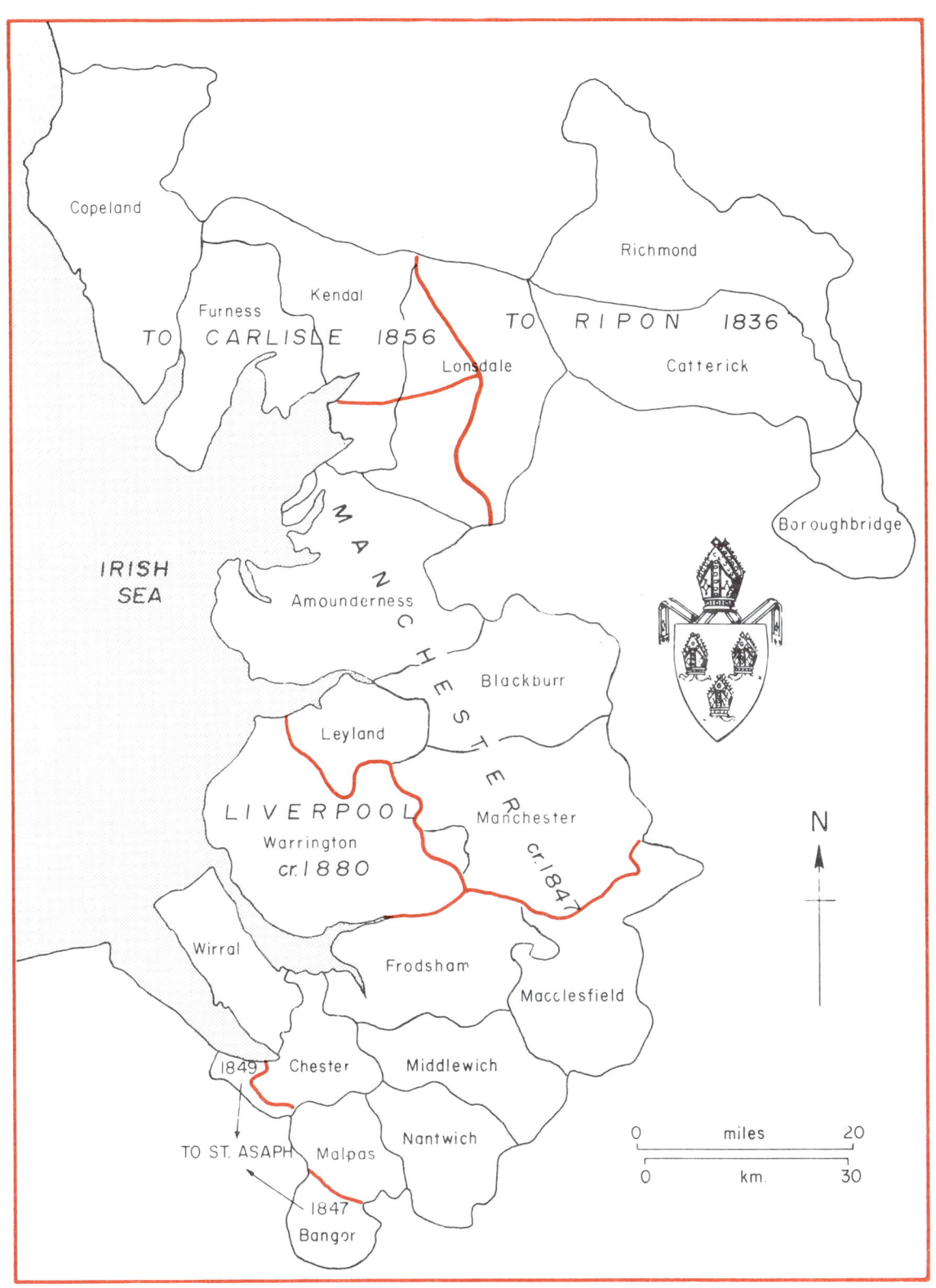

Copeland

Richmond

Furness

Kendal

TO CARLISLE 1856

TO RIPON 1836

Lonsdale

Catterick

Boroughbridge

IRISH SEA

Amounderness

M A N C H E S T E R

Blackburr

Leyland

LIVERPOOL

Manchester

cr.1847

Warrington
cr.1880

N

Wirral

Frodsham

Macclesfield

1849

Chester

Middlewich

TO ST. ASAPH

Malpas

Nantwich

1847

Bangor

0	miles	20
0	km.	30

TOWNSHIPS

The township was, for most purposes, the smallest unit of administration for the period dealt with in this booklet. It was used for judicial, fiscal and military purposes though generally the only officer it possessed was the constable. The earliest comprehensive list of Cheshire townships is found in connection with the collection of the distinctive Cheshire tax, the "Mize", in 1406 (see *VCH Ches* II 23 and 65) though they are clearly in existence long before this. For a general discussion of the township the reader is referred to Helen Jewell *English Local Administration In The Middle Ages* (1972) 60-61 which points out significantly that it is the township rather than the manor "which has entity as a taxable and representable community".

ALPHABETICAL LIST OF TOWNSHIPS

Showing the Parishes, Chapelries, Hundreds
and Deaneries in which they lay.

TOWNSHIP	ANCIENT PARISH AND (CHAPELRY)	HUNDRED	DEANERY
Acton	Acton	NA	NN
Acton	Weaverham	ED	FR
Acton Grange	Runcorn (Daresbury)	BU	FR
Adlington	Prestbury	MA	MC
Agden	Malpas	BR	ML
Agden (part)	Bowden	BU	FR
Agden (part)	Rostherne	BU	FR
Alcumlow, see Moreton			
Alderley, see Nether Alderley, Over Alderley			
Aldersey	Coddington	BR	ML
Aldford	Aldford	BR	ML
Allostock	Great Budworth (Lower Peover)	NO	FR
Alpraham	Bunbury	ED	NN
Alsager	Barthomley (Alsager)	NA	NN
Alstanton, see Austerson			
Altrincham	Bowdon (Altrincham)	BU	FR
Alvanley	Frodsham (Alvanley)	ED	FR
Alvaston	Nantwich	NA	NN
Anderton	Great Budworth	BU	FR
Antrobus	Great Budworth	BU	FR
Appleton al. Hull Appleton	Great Budworth	BU	FR
Arclid	Sandbach	NO	MD
Arrowe	Woodchurch	WI	WR
Ashley	Bowdon	BU	FR
Ashton	Tarvin	ED	CS
Ashton upon Mersey (part, see note 37)	Ashton upon Mersey	BU	FR
Ashton upon Mersey (part, see note 37)	Bowdon	BU	FR
Astbury, see Newbold Astbury			
Aston by Budworth	Great Budworth	BU	FR
Aston by Sutton	Runcorn (Aston)	BU	FR
Aston Grange	Runcorn (Aston)	BU	FR
Aston iuxta Mondrum	Acton	NA	NN
Audlem	Audlem	NA	NN
Austerson al. Alstanton	Acton	NA	NN
Bache	Chester St Oswald	BR	CS
Backford (see note 39)	Backford	WI	WR
Baddiley (see note 5)	Baddiley	NA	NN
Baddington	Acton	NA	NN
Baguley (see note 33)	Bowdon	BU	FR
Balterley (Staffs)	Barthomley		NN

TOWNSHIP	ANCIENT PARISH AND (CHAPELRY)	HUNDRED	DEANERY
Barnshaw, see Goostrey			
Barnston	Woodchurch	WI	WR
Barnton	Great Budworth	BU	FR
Barrow (comprised Great Barrow and Little Barrow)	Barrow	ED	CS
Barthomley	Barthomley	NA	NN
Bartington	Great Budworth	BU	FR
Barton	Farndon	BR	CS
Basford	Wynbunbury	NA	NN
Batherton	Wybunbury	NA	NN
Bebington, see Lower Bebington, Higher Bebington			
Beeston	Bunbury	ED	NN
Betchton	Sandbach	NA	MD
Bexton	Rostherne (Knutsford)	BU	FR
Bickerton	Malpas	BR	ML
Bickley	Malpas	BR	ML
Bidston cum Ford	Bidston	WI	WR
Birches	Great Budworth (Witton)	NO	FR
Birkenhead (see note 32)	Bidston or extra parochial (Birkenhead)	WI	WR
Birtles	Prestbury	MA	MC
Blackden	Sandbach (Goostrey)	NO	MD
Blacon cum Crabwall (Crabwall part, see note 17)	Chester St. Oswald	WI	CS
Blacon cum Crabwall (Blacon part, see note 17)	Chester Holy Trinity	WI	CS
Blakenhall	Wybunbury	NA	NN
Bollin Fee	Wilmslow	MA	MC
Bollington	Prestbury	MA	MC
Bollington (part)	Bowdon	BU	FR
Bollington (part)	Rostherne	BU	FR
Bosden, see Handforth (see note 21)	Cheadle	MA	MC
Bosley	Prestbury (Bosley)	MA	MC
Bostock	Davenham	NO	MD
Boughton, see Great Boughton, Chester: Spital Boughton			
Bowdon	Bowdon	BU	FR
Bradford, see Shurlach			
Bradley al. Welsh Bradley (see note 12)	Malpas	BR	ML
Bradwall	Sandbach	NO	MD
Bramhall	Stockport	MA	MC
Bredbury	Stockport	MA	MC
Brereton cum Smethwick	Brereton	NO	MD
Bridgemere	Wybunbury	NA	NN
Bridge Trafford	Plemstall	ED	CS
Brimstage	Bromborough	WI	WR
Brindley	Acton	NA	NN
Brinnington	Stockport	MA	MC
Bromborough	Bromborough	WI	WR
Broomhall	Acton (Wrenbury)	NA	NN
Broxton	Malpas	BR	ML
Bruen Stapleford	Tarvin	ED	CS
Budworth, see Great Budworth, Little Budworth			
Budworth en le Frith, see Little Budworth			
Buerton	Aldford	BR	ML
Buerton	Audlem	NA	NN

TOWNSHIP	ANCIENT PARISH AND (CHAPELRY)	HUNDRED	DEANERY
Buglawton	Astbury	NO	MD
Bulkeley	Malpas	BR	ML
Bunbury	Bunbury	ED	NN
Burland	Acton	NA	NN
Burton	Tarvin	ED	CS
Burton	Burton	WI	WR
Burwardsley	Bunbury (Burwardsley)	BR	NN
Butley	Prestbury	MA	MC
Byley cum Yatehouse	Middlewich	NO	MD
Caldecott	Shocklach	BR	ML
Caldy, formerly Little Caldy	West Kirby	WI	WR
Caldy Grange, see Grange			
Calveley	Bunbury	ED	NN
Capenhurst	Shotwick	WI	WR
Capesthorne	Prestbury (Capesthorne)	MA	MC
Carden	Tilston	BR	ML
Carrington	Bowdon (Carrington)	BU	FR
Castle Northwich	Great Budworth (Witton)	ED	FR
Caughall	Backford	BR	WR
Chadkirk, see Romiley			
Cheadle Bulkeley	Cheadle	MA	MC
Cheadle Moseley al.	Cheadle	MA	MC
Cheadle Hulme			
Cheaveley, see Huntington			
Checkley cum Wrinehill	Wybunbury	NA	NN
Chelford al. Chelford cum Astle	Prestbury (Chelford)	MA	MC

Chester:-

TOWNSHIP	ANCIENT PARISH AND (CHAPELRY)	HUNDRED	DEANERY
Castle	Extra-parochial	BR	
Cathedral	Extra-parochial		
Gloverstone	St. Mary on the Hill	BR	CS
Holy Trinity			CS
Little St. John (see note 38)	Extra-parochial		
St. Bridget			CS
St. John the Baptist			CS
St. Martin			CS
St. Mary on the Hill			CS
St. Michael			CS
St. Olave			CS
St. Oswald			CS
St. Peter			CS
Spital Boughton al. St Giles Hospital	Extra-parochial		

TOWNSHIP	ANCIENT PARISH AND (CHAPELRY)	HUNDRED	DEANERY
Chidlow	Malpas	BR	ML
Childer Thornton	Eastham	WI	WR
Cholmondeley	Malpas	BR	ML
Cholmondeston	Acton	NA	NN
Chorley	Acton (Wrenbury)	NA	NN
Chorley	Wilmslow	MA	MC
Chorlton	Malpas	BR	ML
Chorlton	Wybunbury	NA	NN
Chorlton by Backford	Backford	WI	WR
Chowley	Coddington	BR	ML
Christleton	Christleton	BR	CS
Church Coppenhall	Coppenhall	NA	NN
Church Hulme al. Holmes Chapel	Sandbach (Church Hulme)	NO	MD
Church Lawton	Church Lawton	NO	MD

TOWNSHIP	ANCIENT PARISH AND (CHAPELRY)	HUNDRED	DEANERY
Church Minshull	Church Minshull	NA	NN
Church Shocklach	Shocklach	BR	ML
Churton by Aldford	Aldford	BR	ML
Churton by Farndon	Farndon	BR	CS
Churton Heath al. Church en Heath	Chester St. Oswald (Bruera)	BR	CS
Claughton cum Grange (greater part, see note 16)	Bidston	WI	WR
Claughton cum Grange (small part, see note 16)	Woodchurch	WI	WR
Claverton	Chester St. Mary on the Hill	BR	CS
Clifton al. Rocksavage	Runcorn	BU	FR
Clive	Middlewich	NO	MD
Clotton Hoofield	Tarvin	ED	CS
Clutton	Farndon	BR	CS
Coddington al. Coddington cum Beachin	Coddington	BR	ML
Cogshall	Great Budworth	BU	FR
Comberbach	Great Budworth	BU	FR
Congleton	Astbury (Congleton)	NO	MD
Coole Pilate (greater part see note 18)	Acton	NA	NN
Coole Pilate (small part, see note 18)	Audlem	NA	NN
Coppenhall, see Church Coppenhall, Monks Coppenhall			
Cotton	Sandbach (Church Hulme)	NO	MD
Cotton Abbotts	Christleton	BR	CS
Cotton Edmunds	Christleton	BR	CS
Crabwall, see Blacon			
Cranage	Sandbach (Church Hulme)	NO	MD
Crewe	Barthomley	NA	NN
Crewe by Farndon	Farndon	BR	CS
Croughton	Chester St. Oswald	WI	CS
Crowley	Great Budworth	BU	FR
Crowton (see note 26)	Weaverham	ED	FR
Croxton	Middlewich	NO	MD
Cuddington al. Kiddington	Malpas	BR	ML
Cuddington	Weaverham	ED	FR
Daresbury	Runcorn (Daresbury)	BU	FR
Darnhall	Whitegate	ED	MD
Davenham	Davenham	NO	MD
Davenport	Astbury	NO	MD
Delamere	Delamere	ED	FR
Disley al. Disley Stanley	Stockport (Disley)	MA	MC
Dodcott cum Wilkesley (part)	Acton (Wrenbury)	NA	NN
Dodcott cum Wilkesley (part)	Audlem	NA	NN
Doddington	Wybunbury	NA	NN
Dodleston	Dodleston	BR	CS
Duckington	Malpas	BR	ML
Duddon	Tarvin	ED	CS
Dukinfield	Stockport	MA	MC
Dunham Massey	Bowdon	BU	FR
Dunham on the Hill	Thornton	ED	CS
Dutton (greater part, see note 27)	Great Budworth	BU	FR
Dutton (part, see note 27)	Runcorn	BU	FR
Earnshaw, see Rudheath (and note 4)			
Eastham al. Eastham cum Plymyard and Carlett	Eastham	WI	WR
Eaton	Astbury	MA	MD
Eaton	Davenham	NO	MD
Eaton	Eccleston	BR	CS

TOWNSHIP	ANCIENT PARISH AND (CHAPELRY)	HUNDRED	DEANERY
Eaton	Tarporley	ED	CS
Eccleston al. Eccleston cum Belgrave	Eccleston	BR	CS
Eddisbury	Delamere	ED	FR
Edge	Malpas	BR	ML
Edgerley	Aldford	BR	ML
Edleston	Acton	NA	NN
Egerton	Malpas	BR	ML
Elton	Thornton	ED	CS
Elton	Warmingham	NO	MD
Etchells, see Northen Etchells, Stockport Etchells			
Faddiley	Acton	NA	NN
Fallibroome	Prestbury	MA	MC
Farndon	Farndon	BR	CS
Ford, see Bidston			
Foulk Stapleford (contains Hargrave Chapel)	Tarvin	BR	CS
Frankby	West Kirby	WI	WR
Frith, see Little Budworth, Wrenbury			
Frodsham	Frodsham	ED	FR
Frodsham Lordship	Frodsham	ED	FR
Fulshaw	Wilmslow	MA	MC
Gawsworth	Gawsworth	MA	MC
Gayton	Heswall	WI	WR
Godley	Mottram in Longdendale	MA	MC
Golborne Bellow	Tattenhall	BR	ML
Golborne David	Handley	BR	ML
Goostrey cum Barnshaw	Sandbach (Goostrey)	NO	MD
Grafton (see note 36)	Tilston (formerly extra parochial)	BR	ML
Grange, formerly Great Caldy or Caldy Grange	West Kirby	WI	WR
Grange, see Claughton			
Grappenhall	Grappenhall	BU	FR
Greasby (greater part)	West Kirby	WI	WR
Greasby (small part)	Thurstaston	WI	WR
Great Barrow, see Barrow			
Great Boughton	Chester St Oswald	BR	CS
Great Budworth	Great Budworth	BU	FR
Great Caldy, see Grange			
Great Meols	West Kirby	WI	WR
Great Mollington al. Mollington Tarrant or Torold	Backford	WI	WR
Great Mouldsworth, seeMouldsworth			
Great Neston	Neston	WI	WR
Great Peover, see Nether Peover			
Great Saughall	Shotwick	WI	WR
Great Stanney	Extra parochial	WI	
Great Sutton	Eastham	WI	WR
Great Warford	Alderley	MA	MC
Gresty, see Shavington			
Grindley, see Tushingham			
Guilden Sutton	Guilden Sutton	BR	CS
Hale	Bowdon	BU	FR
Halton	Runcorn (Halton)	BU	FR
Hampton	Malpas	BR	ML
Handforth cum Bosden (see note 21)	Cheadle	MA	MC

TOWNSHIP	ANCIENT PARISH AND (CHAPELRY)	HUNDRED	DEANERY
Handley	Handley	BR	ML
Hankelow	Audlem	NA	NN
Hapsford	Thornton	ED	CS
Hargrave, see Little Neston			
Hartford	Great Budworth (Witton)	ED	FR
Harthill	Harthill	BR	ML
Haslington	Barthomley (Haslington)	NA	NN
Hassall	Sandbach	NA	MD
Hatherton	Wybunbury	NA	NN
Hattersley	Mottram in Longdendale	MA	MC
Hatton	Runcorn (Daresbury)	BU	FR
Hatton	Waverton	BR	CS
Haughton	Bunbury	ED	NN
Helsby	Frodsham	ED	FR
Henbury cum Pexhall	Prestbury	MA	MC
Henhull	Acton	NA	NN
Heswall cum Oldfield	Heswall	WI	WR
Higher Bebington	Bebington	WI	WR
Higher Kinnerton (Flints.)	Dodleston		CS
Higher Walton, see Walton Superior			
Higher Whitley	Great Budworth	BU	FR
Hilbre (see note 15)	Chester St. Oswald	WI	CS
High Legh	Rostherne	BU	FR
Hockenhull	Tarvin	ED	CS
Hollingworth	Mottram in Longdendale	MA	MC
Holmes Chapel, see Church Hulme			
Hoole (greater part, see note 40)	Plemstall	BR	CS
Hoole (small part, see note 40)	Chester St. John	BR	CS
Hoose	West Kirby	WI	WR
Hooton al. Hooton cum Rivacre	Eastham	WI	WR
Horton	Tilston	BR	ML
Horton cum Peel al. Little Mouldsworth	Tarvin	ED	CS
Hough	Wybunbury	NA	NN
Hull Appleton, see Appleton			
Hulme Walfield	Astbury	NO	MD
Hulme, see Kinderton			
Hulse	Great Budworth (Witton)	NO	FR
Hunsterson	Wybunbury	NA	NN
Huntington al. Huntington cum Cheaveley	Chester St Oswald (Bruera)	BR	CS
Hurdsfield	Prestbury (Macclesfield)	MA	MC
Hurleston	Acton	NA	NN
Huxley	Waverton	BR	CS
Hyde	Stockport	MA	MC
Iddinshall (see note 20)	Chester St. Oswald	ED	CS
Ince (greater part, see note 1)	Ince	ED	CS
Ince (small part, see note 1)	Stoke	ED	WR
Irby (greater part)	Woodchurch	WI	WR
Irby (small part)	Thurstaston	WI	WR
Iscoyd (Flints.)	Malpas (Whitewell)		ML
Keckwick	Runcorn (Daresbury)	BU	FR
Kelsall	Tarvin	ED	CS
Kermincham	Swettenham	NO	MD
Kettleshulme	Prestbury (Macclesfield)	MA	MC
Kiddington, see Cuddington			
Kinderton cum Hulme	Middlewich	NO	MD
Kingsley	Frodsham	ED	FR
King's Marsh al. Overmarsh	Extra parochial	BR	

TOWNSHIP	ANCIENT PARISH AND (CHAPELRY)	HUNDRED	DEANERY
Kingswood	Delamere	ED	FR
Kinnerton, see Higher Kinnerton, Lower Kinnerton			
Knutsford, see Nether Knutsford, Over Knutsford			
Lach Dennis	Great Budworth (Witton)	NO	FR
Lache, see Marlston			
Landican	Woodchurch	WI	WR
Larkton	Malpas	BR	ML
Larton, see Newton			
Latchford	Grappenhall (Latchford)	BU	FR
Lea	Backford	WI	WR
Lea	Wybunbury	NA	NN
Lea Newbold	Chester St. Oswald (Bruera)	BR	CS
Ledsham	Neston	WI	WR
Leese	Sandbach (Goostrey)	NO	MD
Leftwich	Davenham	NO	MD
Leigh, see Little Leigh			
Leighton	Nantwich	NA	NN
Leighton	Neston	WI	WR
Lingham, see Moreton			
Liscard	Wallasey	WI	WR
Little Barrow, see Barrow			
Little Budworth al. Budworth en le Frith	Little Budworth	ED	MD
Little Caldy, see Caldy			
Little Leigh	Great Budworth (Little Leigh)	BU	FR
Little Meols	West Kirby	WI	WR
Little Mollington al. Mollington Banastre	Chester St. Mary on the Hill	WI	CS
Little Mouldsworth, see Horton cum Peel			
Little Neston al. Little Neston cum Hargrave	Neston	WI	WR
Little Peover, see Peover Inferior			
Little Saughall	Shotwick	WI	WR
Little Stanney	Stoke	WI	WR
Little Sutton	Eastham	WI	WR
Littleton	Christleton	BR	CS
Little Warford, see Marthall			
Longdendale, see Mottram in Longdendale			
Lostock Gralam	Great Budworth (Witton)	NO	FR
Lower Bebington	Bebington	WI	WR
Lower Kinnerton	Dodleston	BR	CS
Lower Peover, see Nether Peover			
Lower Walton, see Walton Inferior			
Lower Whitley	Great Budworth (Lower Whitley)	BU	FR
Lower Withington	Prestbury	MA	MC
Lyme Handley	Prestbury	MA	MC
Lymm	Lymm	BU	FR
Macclesfield	Prestbury (Macclesfield)	MA	MC
Macclesfield Forest	Prestbury, (Macclesfield, Macclesfield Forest)	MA	MC
Macefen	Malpas	BR	ML
Malpas	Malpas	BR	ML
Manley	Frodsham	ED	FR
Marbury	Great Budworth	BU	FR
Marbury cum Quoisley	Whitchurch (Marbury)	NA	NN
Marlston cum Lache	Chester St. Mary on the Hill	BR	CS
Marple	Stockport (Marple)	MA	MC

TOWNSHIP	ANCIENT PARISH AND (CHAPELRY)	HUNDRED	DEANERY
Marston (see note 9)	Great Budworth	BU	FR
Marthall with Little Warford	Rostherne (Over Peover)	BU	FR
Marton (see note 29)	Prestbury (Marton)	MA	MC
Marton (greater part)	Whitegate	ED	MD
Marton (small part)	Over	ED	MD
Matley	Mottram in Longdendale	MA	MC
Meols, see Little Meols, Great Meols			
Mere	Rostherne	BU	FR
Mickle Trafford	Plemstall	BR	CS
Middleton Grange (see note 30)	Extra parochial	BU	
Middlewich	Middlewich	NO	MD
Millington	Rostherne	BU	FR
Milton, see Weaverham			
Minshull Vernon	Middlewich	NO	MD
Mobberley	Mobberley	BU	MC
Mollington, see Great Mollington, Little Mollington			
Monks Coppenhall	Coppenhall	NA	NN
Moore	Runcorn (Daresbury)	BU	FR
Mooresbarrow cum Parme	Middlewich	NO	MD
Moreton cum Alcumlow	Astbury	NO	MD
Moreton cum Lingham	Bidston	WI	WR
Moston	Chester St. Mary on the Hill	BR	CS
Moston	Warmingham	NO	MD
Mottram in Longdendale	Mottram in Longdendale	MA	MC
Mottram St. Andrew	Prestbury	MA	MC
Mouldsworth al.Great Mouldsworth	Tarvin	ED	CS
Moulton	Davenham	NO	MD
Nantwich	Nantwich	NA	NN
Ness	Neston	WI	WR
Neston, see Great Neston, Little Neston			
Nether Alderley	Alderley	MA	MC
Nether Knutsford	Rostherne (Knutsford)	BU	FR
Nether Peover al.Lower Peover al.Great Peover	Great Budworth (Lower Peover)	NO	FR
Netherpool	Eastham	WI	WR
Nether Tabley, see Tabley Inferior			
Newbold Astbury	Astbury	NO	MD
Newhall	Davenham	NO	MD
Newhall (part, see notes 6 & 13)	Acton (Wrenbury)	NA	NN
Newhall (part, see notes 6 & 13)	Audlem	NA	NN
Newton	Middlewich	NO	MD
Newton	Mottram in Longdendale	MA	MC
Newton	Prestbury	MA	MC
Newton by Chester	Chester St. Oswald	BR	CS
Newton by Daresbury	Runcorn (Daresbury)	BU	FR
Newton by Frodsham	Frodsham	ED	FR
Newton by Malpas	Malpas	BR	ML
Newton by Tattenhall	Tattenhall	BR	ML
Newton cum Larton	West Kirby	WI	WR
Noctorum	Woodchurch	WI	WR
Norbury	Stockport	MA	MC
Norbury	Whitchurch (Marbury)	NA	NN
Norley (see note 26)	Frodsham	ED	FR
North Rode	Prestbury	MA	MC
Northen Etchells	Northenden	MA	MC
Northenden al. Northen	Northenden	MA	MC
Northwich	Great Budworth (Witton)	NO	FR
Norton	Runcorn	BU	FR

TOWNSHIP	ANCIENT PARISH AND (CHAPELRY)	HUNDRED	DEANERY
Oakmere	Delamere	ED	FR
Occlestone	Middlewich	NO	MD
Odd Rode	Astbury	NO	MD
Offerton	Stockport	MA	MC
Old Withington	Prestbury (Chelford)	MA	MC
Oldcastle	Malpas	BR	ML
Oldfield, see Heswall			
Ollerton	Rostherne (Knutsford)	BU	FR
Onston	Weaverham	ED	FR
Oulton Lowe	Over	ED	MD
Over (part, see note 19)	Over	ED	MD
Over (part, see note 19)	Whitegate	ED	MD
Over Alderley	Alderley	MA	MC
Over Knutsford	Rostherne (Knutsford)	BU	FR
Over Peover, see Peover Superior			
Over Tabley, see Tabley Superior			
Overpool	Eastham	WI	WR
Overton	Malpas	BR	ML
Oxton	Woodchurch	WI	WR
Parme, see Mooresbarrow			
Partington	Bowdon (Carrington)	BU	FR
Peckforton	Bunbury	ED	NN
Peel, see Horton			
Pensby	Woodchurch	WI	WR
Peover, see Nether Peover, Peover Inferior, Peover Superior			
Peover Inferior al. Little Peover	Great Budworth (Lower Peover)	BU	FR
Peover Superior al. Over Peover	Rostherne (Over Peover)	BU	FR
Pexhall, see Henbury			
Pickmere	Great Budworth	BU	FR
Picton	Plemstall	BR	CS
Plumley	Great Budworth (Lower Peover)	BU	FR
Poole	Acton	NA	NN
Pott Shrigley	Prestbury (Macclesfield, Pott Shrigley)	MA	MC
Poulton	Pulford	BR	CS
Poulton cum Seacombe	Wallasey	WI	WR
Poulton cum Spital al. Poulton Lancelyn	Bebington	WI	WR
Pownall Fee	Wilmslow	MA	MC
Poynton	Prestbury (Poynton)	MA	MC
Prenton	Woodchurch	WI	WR
Prestbury	Prestbury	MA	MC
Preston on the Hill	Runcorn (Daresbury)	BU	FR
Prior's Heys	Extra-parochial	ED	
Puddington	Burton	WI	WR
Pulford	Pulford	BR	CS
Quoisley, see Marbury cum Quoisley			
Raby	Neston	WI	WR
Radnor	Astbury	NO	MD
Rainow	Prestbury (Macclesfield, Rainow)	MA	MC
Ravenscroft	Middlewich	NO	MD
Ridley	Bunbury	ED	NN
Rocksavage, see Clifton			
Rode see North Rode, Odd Rode			
Romiley al. Chadkirk	Stockport (Chadkirk)	MA	MC

TOWNSHIP	ANCIENT PARISH AND (CHAPELRY)	HUNDRED	DEANERY
Rope	Wybunbury	NA	NN
Rostherne	Rostherne	BU	FR
Rough Shotwick, see Woodbank			
Rowton	Christleton	BR	CS
Rudheath Lordship (greater part, see note 11)	Davenham or Extra-parochial	NO	MD
Rudheath Lordship (small part, see note 11)	Great Budworth (Witton) or Extra-parochial	NO	FR
Rudheath Lordship (Earnshaw see note 4)	Sandbach or Extra-parochial	NO	MD
Runcorn	Runcorn	BU	FR
Rushton	Tarporley	ED	CS
Saighton	Chester St. Oswald (Bruera)	BR	CS
Sale	Ashton upon Mersey	BU	FR
Sandbach	Sandbach	NO	MD
Saughall, see Great Saughall, Little Saughall			
Saughall Massie	Bidston	WI	WR
Seacombe, see Poulton			
Seven Oaks	Great Budworth	BU	FR
Shavington cum Gresty	Wybunbury	NA	NN
Shipbrook	Davenham	NO	MD
Shocklach, see Church Shocklach, Shocklach Oviatt			
Shocklach Oviatt	Shocklach	BR	ML
Shotwick	Shotwick	WI	WR
Shotwick Park	Extra parochial	WI	
Shurlach cum Bradford	Davenham	NO	MD
Siddington	Prestbury (Siddington)	MA	MC
Smallwood	Astbury	NO	MD
Smethwick, see Brereton			
Snelson	Rostherne (Over Peover)	MA	FR
Somerford al. Somerford Radnor	Astbury	NO	MD
Somerford Booths	Astbury	MA	MD
Sound (part)	Acton	NA	NN
Sound (part)	Acton (Wrenbury)	NA	NN
Spital, see Poulton, Chester: Spital Boughton			
Sproston	Middlewich	NO	MD
Spurstow	Bunbury	ED	NN
Stanlow (see note 2)	Extra parochial	WI	
Stanney, see Great Stanney, Little Stanney			
Stanthorne	Davenham	NO	MD
Stapeley	Wybunbury	NA	NN
Stapleford, see Bruen Stapleford Foulk Stapleford			
Stayley	Mottram in Longdendale	MA	MC
Stockham	Runcorn	BU	FR
Stockport	Stockport	MA	MC
Stockport Etchells	Stockport	MA	MC
Stockton	Malpas	BR	ML
Stockton Heath (see note 28)			
Stoke	Acton	NA	NN
Stoke	Stoke	WI	WR
Storeton	Bebington	WI	WR
Stretton	Great Budworth	BU	FR
Stretton	Tilston	BR	ML
Stublach (see note 10)	Middlewich	NO	MD
Sutton, see Great Sutton, Guilden Sutton, Little Sutton			
Sutton	Middlewich	NO	MD
Sutton al. Sutton Downes	Prestbury (Macclesfield)	MA	MC
Sutton iuxta Frodsham	Runcorn (Aston)	BU	FR
Swettenham	Swettenham	NO	MD

TOWNSHIP	ANCIENT PARISH AND (CHAPELRY)	HUNDRED	DEANERY
Tabley Inferior al. Nether Tabley	Great Budworth	BU	FR
Tabley Superior al. Over Tabley cum Sudlow	Rostherne	BU	FR
Tarporley	Tarporley	ED	CS
Tarvin al. Tarvin cum Oscroft	Tarvin	ED	CS
Tattenhall	Tattenhall	BR	ML
Tatton	Rostherne	BU	FR
Taxal	Taxal	MA	MC
Tetton	Warmingham	NO	MD
Thelwall	Runcorn (Daresbury, Thelwall)	BU	FR
Thingwall	Woodchurch	WI	WR
Thornton Hough al. Thornton Mayo	Neston	WI	WR
Thornton le Moors	Thornton	ED	CS
Threapwood (part in Flints.)	Extra parochial		
Thurstaston	Thurstaston	WI	WR
Tilston	Tilston	BR	ML
Tilstone Fearnall	Bunbury	ED	NN
Timperley	Bowdon	BU	FR
Tintwistle	Mottram in Longdendale	MA	MC
Tittenley al. Titley	Audlem	NA	NN
Tiverton	Bunbury	ED	NN
Toft	Rostherne (Knutsford)	BU	FR
Torkington	Stockport	MA	MC
Trafford, see Bridge Trafford, Mickle Trafford, Wimbolds Trafford			
Tranmere	Bebington	WI	WR
Tushingham cum Grindley	Malpas	BR	ML
Twambrook, see Witton			
Twemlow (see note 14)	Sandbach (Goostrey)	NO	MD
Tytherington	Prestbury	MA	MC
Upton (greater part)	Chester St. Mary on the Hill	BR	CS
Upton (small part)	Chester St. Oswald	BR	CS
Upton	Overchurch	WI	WR
Upton	Prestbury	MA	MC
Utkinton	Tarporley	ED	CS
Walgherton	Wybunbury	NA	NN
Wallasey	Wallasey	WI	WR
Wallerscote	Weaverham	ED	FR
Walton Inferior al. Lower Walton	Runcorn (Daresbury)	BU	FR
Walton Superior al. Higher Walton	Runcorn (Daresbury)	BU	FR
Warburton	Warburton	BU	FR
Wardle	Bunbury	ED	NN
Warford, see Great Warford, Little Warford			
Warmingham	Warmingham	NO	MD
Waverton al. Warton	Waverton	BR	CS
Weaver	Middlewich	ED	MD
Weaverham cum Milton (see note 25)	Weaverham	ED	FR
Werneth	Stockport	MA	MC
Wervin	Chester St. Oswald	BR	CS
West Kirby	West Kirby	WI	WR
Weston	Runcorn	BU	FR
Weston	Wybunbury	NA	NN
Wettenhall	Over (Wettenhall)	ED	MD
Whaley, see Yeardsley			
Wharton	Davenham	NO	MD
Whatcroft	Davenham	NO	MD
Wheelock	Sandbach	NO	MD
Whitby (part, see note 3)	Eastham	WI	WR
Whitby (part, see note 3)	Stoke	WI	WR

TOWNSHIP	ANCIENT PARISH AND (CHAPELRY)	HUNDRED	DEANERY
Whitley, see Higher Whitley, Lower Whitley			
Wigland	Malpas	BR	ML
Wildboarclough	Prestbury (Macclesfield)	MA	MC
Wilkesley, see Dodcott			
Willaston	Neston	WI	WR
Willaston (part)	Nantwich	NA	NN
Willaston (part)	Wybunbury	NA	NN
Willington	Extra parochial	ED	
Wimboldsley	Middlewich	NO	MD
Wimbolds Trafford	Thornton	ED	CS
Wincham	Great Budworth	BU	FR
Wincle	Prestbury (Macclesfield, Wincle)	MA	MC
Winnington	Great Budworth (Witton)	ED	FR
Wirswall	Whitchurch, Salop	NA	
Wistaston	Wistaston	NA	NN
Withington, see Lower Withington, Old Withington			
Witton cum Twambrook	Great Budworth (Witton)	NO	FR
Woodbank al. Rough Shotwick	Shotwick	WI	WR
Woodchurch	Woodchurch	WI	WR
Woodcott	Acton (Wrenbury)	NA	NN
Woodford (see note 31)	Prestbury	MA	MC
Woolstanwood	Nantwich	NA	NN
Worleston	Acton	NA	NN
Worth	Prestbury (Poynton)	MA	MC
Wrenbury cum Frith	Acton (Wrenbury)	NA	NN
Wrinehill, see Checkley			
Wybunbury	Wybunbury	NA	NN
Wychough	Malpas	BR	ML
Yatehouse, see Byley			
Yeardsley cum Whaley	Taxal	MA	MC

PARISHES, CHAPELRIES, TOWNSHIPS AND CHAPELS

The definition of a parish given by Canon J S Purvis in his *Dictionary of Ecclesiastical Terms* (1962) is as succinct as any: "The general name in England for the area which forms the separate spiritual charge of a priest of the church of England known as the incumbent..... that is the person in charge or with "cure of souls". Though existing originally for ecclesiastical purposes the parishes acquired secular functions in later periods like registration after 1538, and most notably under the Elizabethan poor law of 1597.

The enormous size of some of the Cheshire parishes gave rise, as has already been said, to a whole range of subordinate chapelries and chapels. All are included in the following list with the exception of purely domestic chapels, of which there is an interesting early list in Leycester. Domestic chapels which have, at some time, been regarded as chapels of ease have been mentioned, however. The fluctuating status of many of the chapels makes neat categorization difficult as will be apparent from the list. The extent to which the "private" chapel of Cholmondeley for instance could be called simply a domestic chapel (which it generally is) may be left to the reader to judge. It has an extant licence from the dual rectors of Malpas as early as 1285. A petition of c.1320 asks for virtual parochial status. By the nineteenth century it had 51 private sittings and 347 free seats. On the other hand several of the undoubted chapels of ease like Chadkirk, Lower Whitley and Ringway all fell under non-conformist control shortly after the Restoration as did Wettenhall Chapel as late as 1692 (*VCH Ches* III 47). All were pulled back into the established fold at a later date.

The list will be found to show churches and chapels in all stages of evolution towards regularization and independence, from the virtually independent parochial chapelries downwards. It should be stated that the so called "free chapels" like Harthill, Little Budworth and Marton are not Royal Free Chapels of the kind found, for instance, in Staffordshire. The designation seems to be rather an attempt to express a degree of independence even greater than that of the parochial chapelry. The definitions of chapels of ease, parochial chapels and so forth, found in Burns *Ecclesiastical Law* (1763), and the earlier writers cited therein, are a useful starting point, but the touchstone of burial, baptism and administration of the sacraments, "the true distinct parochial rights", is easier to apply in theory than in practice, especially when factors such as the right to tithes and proper discernable assigned districts are taken into account. The status of many Cheshire chapels often seems to depend on opinion, repute and the opportunistic ambitions of clergy and patrons at different times.

Though the booklet deals essentially with jurisdictions rather than buildings, it is worth remembering that chapel status need not necessarily imply an inferior building, indeed the chapels of Nantwich (Acton) and Witton (Great Budworth) are two of the county's most magnificent medieval buildings while Congleton (Astbury) and Macclesfield, Christ Church (a chapel of ease to a chapelry of Prestbury) are notable eighteenth century examples.

PARISHES AND CHAPELRIES WITH THEIR TOWNSHIPS

ACTON

1	Acton	10	Faddiley
2	Aston iuxta Mondrem	11	Henhull
3	Austerson	12	Hurleston
4	Baddington	13	Newhall (small parts, see notes 6 and 13)
5	Brindley	14	Poole
6	Burland	15	Sound (part)
7	Cholmondeston	16	Stoke
8	Coole Pilate (greater part, see note 18)	17	Worleston
9	Edleston		

and some small detached portions of Dodcott cum Wilkesley, Newhall and Baddiley (see notes 5 and 6)

Previously included the parochial chapelries of Church Minshull, Nantwich and Wrenbury, and probably the parish of Baddiley.

ALDERLEY

1	Great Warford	3	Over Alderley
2	Nether Alderley		

Anciently a parochial chapelry of Prestbury, independent by 1328 (Orm III 565, 568).

ALDFORD

1	Aldford	3	Churton by Aldford
2	Buerton	4	Edgerley

ALSAGER CHAPELRY

See under Barthomley. The chapel erected in 1789-90 at the expense of Mary, Margaret and Judith Alsager. Established as a chapel of ease to Barthomley by Act of Parliament 29 Geo. III cap.XI. The township of Alsager was not officially assigned to the chapel until an Order in Council of 1852.

ALTRINCHAM CHAPELRY

See under Bowdon. Created 1799, but a parochial chapel on 1740 map, which may be an allusion to "Booth's Chapel ...... erected about the Reign of Edward IV" (Gastrell).

ALVANLEY CHAPELRY

See under Frodsham

ASHTON UPON MERSEY

1	Ashton upon Mersey (part, see note 37)	2	Sale

An independent rectory by 1350 supposed to have originally been part of Bowdon parish.

ASTBURY

1	Buglawton	7	Newbold Astbury
2	Congleton (Chapelry)	8	Odd Rode
3	Davenport	9	Radnor
4	Eaton	10	Smallwood
5	Hulme Walfield	11	Somerford
6	Moreton cum Alcumlow	12	Somerford Booths

Originally included the parishes of Church Lawton, Brereton and Swettenham.

ASTON CHAPELRY

1	Aston by Sutton with Middleton Grange (see note 30)		
2	Aston Grange	3	Sutton iuxta Frodsham

Formerly in Runcorn parish. Made a parochial chapel 1635 (Leycester).

AUDLEM

1	Audlem	5	Hankelow
2	Buerton	6	Newhall (part, see notes 6 and 13)
3	Coole Pilate (small part see note 18)	7	Tittenley
4	Dodcott cum Wilkesley (parts)		

Probably formed out of Wybunbury parish.

BACKFORD

1	Backford (see note 39)	4	Great Mollington
2	Caughall	5	Lea
3	Chorlton by Backford		

Moston, later in parish of Chester St Mary on the Hill, was originally in Backford Parish.

BADDILEY

1 Baddiley

Probably originally part of Acton parish, possibly of Wybunbury (see note 5).

BARROW

1 Barrow

Comprised the hamlets of Great Barrow and Little Barrow. There was a tradition that it originally formed part of the parish of Tarvin (Gastrell 125).

BARTHOMLEY

1	Alsager (chapelry)	4	Crewe
2	Balterley (Staffs)	5	Haslington (chapelry)
3	Barthomley		

A small part of Hassall is said to have belonged to this parish (Orm III 299).

BEBINGTON

1	Higher Bebington	4	Storeton
2	Lower Bebington	5	Tranmere
3	Poulton cum Spital		

Bebington was a parish church by 1291.

BIDSTON

1	Bidston cum Ford	4	Moreton cum Lingham (a chapel of ease shown on 1740 map but "demolished above 30 years agoe" according to Gastrell).
2	Birkenhead (Chapelry, see note 32)		
3	Claughton cum Grange (see note 16)	5	Saughall Massie

BIRKENHEAD CHAPELRY

See under Bidston and note 32.

BOSLEY CHAPELRY

See under Prestbury. Several rights associated with a parochial chapelry seem to have been conferred by a Papal Bull of 1402 (Orm III 738).

BOWDON

1	Agden (part)	6	Bollington (part)
2	Altrincham (chapelry)	7	Bowdon
3	Ashton on Mersey (part, see note 37)	8	Dunham Massey
4	Ashley	9	Hale (contains Ringway Chapel)
5	Baguley (see note 33)	10	Timperley

Anciently included the parish of Ashton upon Mersey and Carrington chapelry.

BRERETON
1 Brereton cum Smethwick

Originally part of Astbury parish (Orm I 400 and III 81-92). Built about time of Richard I and made a parish church temp. Henry VIII (Leycester).

BROMBOROUGH
1 Brimstage   2 Bromborough

Anciently included Eastham parish.

BRUERA CHAPELRY
1	Churton Heath	3	Lea Newbold
2	Huntington	4	Saighton

A chapelry of the parish of Chester St Oswald.

BUNBURY
1	Alpraham	7	Peckforton
2	Beeston	8	Ridley
3	Bunbury	9	Spurstow
4	Burwardsley (chapelry)	10	Tilstone Fearnall
5	Calveley	11	Tiverton
6	Haughton	12	Wardle

Tarporley seems originally to have been part of Bunbury parish.

BURTON
1 Burton   2 Puddington

BURWARDSLEY CHAPELRY
See under Bunbury, created 1735.

CAPESTHORNE CHAPELRY
See under Prestbury, created 1722.

CARRINGTON CHAPELRY
1 Carrington   2 Partington

Originally part of Bowdon parish. Carrington chapel consecrated 1759.

CHADKIRK CHAPELRY
See PNC I, 292, and under Stockport, Romiley township.

CHEADLE
1 Cheadle Bulkeley (see note 22)   3 Handforth cum Bosden (see note 21)
2 Cheadle Moseley (see note 22)

CHELFORD CHAPELRY
1 Chelford   2 Old Withington

The chapel at Chelford existed from at least 1265/6 (Orm III 711). It was a chapelry of Prestbury. Gastrell states "Made Parochial an.1674".

CHESTER HOLY TRINITY
1 Blacon cum Crabwall (part, see note 17)   2 Holy Trinity (Chester)

CHESTER ST BRIDGET
No dependent townships.

CHESTER ST JOHN
No dependent townships but included part of Hoole.
See note 40 and later Spital Boughton q.v

CHESTER ST MARTIN
No dependent townships.

CHESTER ST MARY ON THE HILL
1	Claverton	4	Moston	
2	Little Mollington	5	St Mary, Chester (incl. Gloverstone)	
3	Marlston cum Lache	6	Upton (greater part)	

See note 24.

CHESTER ST MICHAEL
No dependent townships.

CHESTER ST OLAVE
No dependent townships.

CHESTER ST OSWALD
1	Bache	6	Iddinshall (see note 20)
2	Blacon cum Crabwall (part, see note 17)	7	Newton by Chester
3	Croughton	8	St. Oswald (Chester)
4	Great Boughton	9	Upton (small part)
5	Hilbre (see note 15)	10	Wervin (the lost chapel of Wervin was still designated a chapel of ease on 1740 map. Leycester notes that it had a font in it up to the Civil War "whereby it may be seen to have beene a Parochial Chapel").

See note 23. Bruera chapelry formed part of this parish.

CHESTER ST PETER
No dependent townships.

CHRISTLETON
1	Christleton	4	Littleton
2	Cotton Abbotts	5	Rowton
3	Cotton Edmunds		

CHURCH HULME CHAPELRY
1	Church Hulme	3	Cranage
2	Cotton		

A parochial chapelry of Sandbach.

CHURCH LAWTON
1   Church Lawton

Originally part of Astbury parish.

CHURCH MINSHULL
1   Church Minshull

Formerly a chapelry of Acton parish (Orm III 336, 341).

CODDINGTON
1	Aldersey	3	Coddington
2	Chowley		

CONGLETON CHAPELRY
See under Astbury. Gastrell states "no Wardens nor Parochial Rights" but burial rights granted by Bishop Cartwright in 1687 (Gastrell 239, note).

COPPENHALL
1	Church Coppenhall	2	Monks Coppenhall

Originally a chapelry of Wybunbury parish becoming a separate parish in 1373 (Orm III 326).

DARESBURY CHAPELRY

1	Acton Grange	6	Newton by Daresbury
2	Daresbury	7	Preston on the Hill
3	Hatton	8	Thelwall (chapelry, detached)
4	Keckwick	9	Walton Inferior
5	Moore	10	Walton Superior

A parochial chapelry of Runcorn parish (*VCH Ches* I 243-4).

DAVENHAM

1	Bostock	7	Rudheath Lordship (greater part, see note11)
2	Davenham	8	Shipbrook
3	Eaton	9	Shurlach cum Bradford
4	Leftwich	10	Stanthorne
5	Moulton	11	Wharton
6	Newhall	12	Whatcroft

DELAMERE

1	Delamere	3	Kingswood
2	Eddisbury	4	Oakmere

Parish created in 1812 by Act of Parliament out of the last remaining part of the Forest of Delamere (52 Geo III cap. CXXXVI).

DISLEY CHAPELRY

See under Stockport. The chapel was built in 1512 and consecrated in 1558, becoming a parochial chapelry of Stockport (Orm. III 834).

DODLESTON

1	Dodleston	3	Lower Kinnerton
2	Higher Kinnerton (Flints)		

EASTHAM

1	Childer Thornton	5	Little Sutton
2	Eastham	6	Netherpool
3	Great Sutton	7	Overpool
4	Hooton	8	Whitby (part, see note 3)

In existence by 1152 as a chapelry of Bromborough parish.

ECCLESTON

1	Eaton	2	Eccleston

FARNDON

1	Barton	4	Crewe
2	Churton by Farndon	5	Farndon
3	Clutton		

Up to early 14th cent. Farndon included the chapelry of Holt (Denbighs.)
(See *VCH Ches* I 265-6).

FRODSHAM

1	Alvanley (chapelry)	5	Kingsley
2	Frodsham	6	Manley
3	Frodsham Lordship	7	Newton by Frodsham
4	Helsby	8	Norley (see note 26)

Frodsham included the hamlets of Bradley, Netherton, Overton and Woodhouses, which in some early records are accorded almost township status. Frodsham township and Frodsham Lordship are intermixed to an extent which makes reference to the O.S. essential.

GAWSWORTH
1   Gawsworth

A chapelry of Prestbury parish becoming independent in 1382 (Orm III 556). For Mutlow see note 29.

GOOSTREY CHAPELRY
1   Blackden

2   Goostrey cum Barnshaw

3   Leese (see note 34)

4   Twemlow (see note 14)

Established as a parochial chapelry of Sandbach parish by 1350.

GRAPPENHALL
1   Grappenhall

2   Latchford (chapelry)

GREAT BUDWORTH
1   Anderton

2   Antrobus

3   Appleton

4   Aston by Budworth

5   Barnton

6   Bartington

7   Cogshall

8   Comberbach

9   Crowley

10   Dutton (greater part, see note 27)

11   Great Budworth

12   Higher Whitley

13   Little Leigh (chapelry)

14   Lower Whitley (chapelry)

15   Marbury

16   Marston (see note 9)

17   Pickmere

18   Seven Oaks

19   Stretton "very ruinous and in decay" (Gastrell) but shown as a chapel of ease. (1740 map).

20   Tabley Inferior

21   Wincham

The parochial chapelries of Lower Peover and Witton belonged to Great Budworth.

GUILDEN SUTTON
1   Guilden Sutton

HALTON CHAPELRY
See under Runcorn, though EDV 7/1/127, implies that it included the townships of Norton and Stockham as well as Halton. Episcopal licence for divine service in 1398 (Orm I 710).

HANDLEY
1   Golborne David

2   Handley

HARTHILL
1   Harthill

Harthill was a "free chapelry", probably originally part of Malpas parish.

HASLINGTON CHAPELRY
See under Barthomley. In existence by 1302 (Gastrell 214).

HESWALL
1   Gayton

2   Heswall cum Oldfield

INCE
1   Ince (see note 1)

KNUTSFORD CHAPELRY
1   Bexton

2   Nether Knutsford "distinct Chappell .. but not a Chappelry" (Gastrell), chapel of ease (1740 map)

3   Ollerton

4   Over Knutsford

5   Toft

Created a parish in 1741 by Act of Parliament 14 Geo. II cap. V and was originally part of Rostherne parish (PNC II 72).

LATCHFORD CHAPELRY
See under Grappenhall, created 1777.

LITTLE BUDWORTH CHAPELRY
1   Little Budworth

First a "free" and then a parochial chapelry in Over parish (PNC III 184).

LITTLE LEIGH CHAPELRY
See under Great Budworth.

LOWER PEOVER CHAPELRY
1	Allostock	3	Peover Inferior
2	Nether Peover	4	Plumley

A parochial chapelry of Great Budworth parish. Chapel built c.1269 (Leycester).

LOWER WHITLEY CHAPELRY
See under Great Budworth.

LYMM
1   Lymm

MACCLESFIELD CHAPELRY
1	Hurdsfield	6	Rainow (chapelry, also contains Jenkin Chapel, Saltersford)
2	Kettleshulme		
3	Macclesfield	7	Sutton Downes
4	Macclesfield Forest (chapelry)	8	Wildboarclough
5	Pott Shrigley (chapelry)	9	Wincle (chapelry)

Established as a parochial chapelry of Prestbury parish in 1278 (Orm. III 751). Christ Church, Macclesfield was erected in 1775 at the expense of Charles Roe. It was established as a chapel of ease to the ancient chapel of St. Michael by Act of Parliament 19 Geo. III cap. VII and consecrated 1779.

MACCLESFIELD FOREST CHAPELRY
See under Macclesfield (Orm. III 770). The curate in 1789 stated that "the Chapelry includes Macclesfield Forest and Wildboar-Clough" (EDV 7/2/102).

MALPAS
1	Agden	13	Egerton
2	Bickerton	14	Hampton
3	Bickley	15	Iscoyd (In Whitewell Chapelry Flints)
4	Bradley (see note 12)	16	Larkton
5	Broxton	17	Macefen
6	Bulkeley	18	Malpas
7	Chidlow	19	Newton by Malpas
8	Cholmondeley (accorded the status of a chapel of ease by Leycester)	20	Oldcastle
		21	Overton
9	Chorlton	22	Stockton
10	Cuddington	23	Tushingham cum Grindley (contains Chad Chapel)
11	Duckington		
12	Edge	24	Wigland
		25	Wychough

Harthill was probably originally part of this parish.

MARBURY CHAPELRY
1	Marbury cum Quoisley	2	Norbury

A parochial chapelry of Whitchurch (Salop) made a parish in 1870.

MARPLE CHAPELRY
See under Stockport.

MARTON CHAPELRY
See under Prestbury. Referred to as the "Free Chapel of Marton" in 1549 (Orm. III 726). For Mutlow see note 29.

MIDDLEWICH
1	Byley cum Yatehouse	9	Occlestone
2	Clive	10	Ravenscroft
3	Croxton	11	Sproston
4	Kinderton cum Hulme	12	Stublach (detached, see note 10)
5	Middlewich	13	Sutton
6	Minshull Vernon	14	Weaver
7	Mooresbarrow cum Parme	15	Wimboldsley
8	Newton		

MOBBERLEY
1   Mobberley

MOTTRAM IN LONGDENDALE
1	Godley	5	Mottram in Longdendale
2	Hattersley	6	Newton
3	Hollingworth	7	Stayley
4	Matley	8	Tintwistle (contains Woodhead Chapel)

Tintwistle includes the hamlets of Micklehurst and Arnfield.

NANTWICH
1	Alvaston	4	Willaston (part)
2	Leighton	5	Woolstanwood
3	Nantwich		

Became a separate parish in 1677 formerly a parochial chapelry of Acton.

NESTON
1	Great Neston	5	Ness
2	Ledsham	6	Raby
3	Leighton	7	Thornton Hough
4	Little Neston cum Hargrave	8	Willaston

NORTHENDEN
1	Northenden	2	Northen Etchells

Also included about 30 fields in Baguley township (see note 33).

OVER
1	Marton (small part)	3	Over (part, see note 19)
2	Oulton Lowe	4	Wettenhall (chapelry)

Over parish was previously much more extensive including Little Budworth chapelry and the parish of Whitegate (see note 19).

OVERCHURCH
1   Upton

OVER PEOVER CHAPELRY
1	Marthall cum Warford	3	Snelson
2	Peover Superior		

A parochial chapelry of Rostherne parish.

PLEMSTALL
1	Bridge Trafford	3	Mickle Trafford
2	Hoole (greater part, see note 40)	4	Picton

POTT SHRIGLEY CHAPELRY

See under Macclesfield. Downes chapel here was mentioned in 1472 (PNC I 134).

POYNTON CHAPELRY

1	Poynton	2	Worth

Original foundation of Poynton chapel probably 1312 when it was recognised as a dependency of Prestbury (Orm. III 684) For the possible inclusion of Woodford in the chapelry see note 31.

PRESTBURY

1	Adlington	11	Marton (chapelry)
2	Birtles	12	Mottram St. Andrew
3	Bollington	13	Newton (chapel of ease 1740 map)
4	Bosley (chapelry)		"entirely ruined" (Gastrell)
5	Butley	14	North Rode
6	Capesthorne (chapelry)	15	Prestbury
7	Fallibroome	16	Siddington (chapelry)
8	Henbury cum Pexall	17	Tytherington
9	Lower Withington	18	Upton
10	Lyme Handley	19	Woodford (see note 31)

The ancient parish originally included the parishes of Alderley, Gawsworth and Taxal and the chapelries of Chelford, Macclesfield and Poynton.

PULFORD

1	Poulton	2	Pulford

RAINOW CHAPELRY

See under Macclesfield.

ROSTHERNE

1	Agden (part)	5	Millington
2	Bollington (part)	6	Rostherne
3	High Legh (chapel of ease 1740 map).	7	Tabley Superior (chapel of ease 1740 map).
4	Mere	8	Tatton

It formerly included the parochial chapelries of Knutsford and Over Peover. Leycester notes the "Chapel in the Street" at Tabley Superior built about the reign of Henry VI "now in great decay".

RUNCORN

1	Clifton	5	Runcorn
2	Dutton (part, see note 27)	6	Stockham
3	Halton (chapelry)	7	Weston
4	Norton		

It formerly included the parochial chapelries of Aston and Daresbury and the lost chapelry of Poolsey (see note 27). The origins of the parish have been discussed by Dr A T Thacker (*VCH Ches* I 253-4).

SANDBACH

1	Arclid	5	Hassall
2	Betchton	6	Sandbach
3	Bradwall	7	Wheelock
4	Earnshaw (a detached part of Rudheath Lordship, see note 4)		

It formerly included the chapelries of Church Hulme and Goostrey.

SHOCKLACH

1	Caldecott	3	Shocklach Oviatt
2	Church Shocklach		

SHOTWICK

1	Capenhurst	4	Shotwick
2	Great Saughall	5	Woodbank
3	Little Saughall		

Shotwick Park (extra-parochial) may originally have been in this parish.

SIDDINGTON CHAPELRY

See under Prestbury.

STOCKPORT

1	Bramhall	8	Norbury(contained Norbury chapel)
2	Bredbury	9	Offerton
3	Brinnington	10	Romiley (Chadkirk Chapelry)
4	Disley (chapelry)	11	Stockport
5	Dukinfield (a chapel of ease, Leycester, and on 1740 map)	12	Stockport Etchells
		13	Torkington
6	Hyde	14	Werneth
7	Marple (chapelry)		

St. Peter's church, Stockport was erected in 1766 at the expense of William Wright. It was established as a chapel of ease to St. Mary's by Act of Parliament 8 Geo. III cap 36 and consecrated in 1768.

STOKE

1	Little Stanney	3	Whitby (part, see note 3)
2	Stoke		

Also small portions of Backford and Ince (see notes 1,3 and 39).

SWETTENHAM

1	Kermincham	2	Swettenham

Probably taken out of Astbury parish.

TARPORLEY

1	Eaton	3	Tarporley
2	Rushton	4	Utkinton

Emerges as a separate parish c.1200 after rejection by the Papal authorities of a claim that it was a chapelry of Bunbury (G Barraclough *Early Cheshire Charters* (1957) 28-9).

TARVIN

1	Ashton	7	Hockenhull
2	Bruen Stapleford	8	Horton cum Peel
3	Burton	9	Kelsall
4	Clotton Hoofield	10	Mouldsworth
5	Duddon	11	Tarvin
6	Foulk Stapleford (contains Hargrave Chapel a parochial chapel in Gastrell and 1740 map)		

Prior's Heys though anciently extra parochial is sometimes taken as part of Tarvin township. May have included the parish of Barrow q.v.

TATTENHALL

1	Golborne Bellow	3	Tattenhall
2	Newton by Tattenhall		

TAXAL

1	Taxal	2	Yeardsley cum Whaley

Taxal was a chapelry of Prestbury parish until 1377 (Orm III 782).

THELWALL CHAPELRY
See under Daresbury.

THORNTON

1	Dunham on the Hill	4	Thornton le Moors
2	Elton	5	Wimbolds Trafford
3	Hapsford		

THURSTASTON

1	Greasby (small part, called "Irby Millhill", Gastrell)	3	Thurstaston
2	Irby (small part)		

TILSTON

1	Carden	4	Stretton
2	Grafton (formerly extra parochial, see note 36)	5	Tilston
3	Horton		

WALLASEY

1	Liscard	3	Wallasey
2	Poulton cum Seacombe		

WARBURTON

1   Warburton

See note 35.

WARMINGHAM

1	Elton	3	Tetton
2	Moston	4	Warmingham

WAVERTON

1	Hatton	3	Waverton
2	Huxley		

WEAVERHAM

1	Acton	4	Onston
2	Crowton (see note 26)	5	Wallerscote
3	Cuddington	6	Weaverham cum Milton (see note 25)

Also said to have contained a small part of Norley (see note 26).

WEST KIRBY

1	Caldy	6	Hoose
2	Frankby	7	Little Meols
3	Grange	8	Newton cum Larton
4	Greasby (greater part)	9	West Kirby
5	Great Meols		

WETTENHALL CHAPELRY
See under Over

WHITEGATE

1	Darnhall	3	Over (part, see note 19)
2	Marton (greater part)		

Parts of Weaverham also belonged to Whitegate parish (see note 25). The parish was created out of Over by Statute 33 Henry VIII cap. 32 in 1541/2. It was also known at first as New Church (see notes 7, 19 and 25).

WILMSLOW

1	Bollin Fee	3	Fulshaw
2	Chorley	4	Pownall Fee

Wilmslow is the name of the church and churchyard extended to the old village (PNC I 219-220).

WINCLE CHAPELRY

See under Macclesfield (Orm. III 769).

WISTASTON

1   Wistaston

Originally part of Wybunbury parish, it became independent c.1299-1300.

WITTON CHAPELRY

1	Birches	6	Lostock Gralam
2	Castle Northwich	7	Northwich
3	Hartford	8	Winnington
4	Hulse	9	Witton cum Twambrook
5	Lach Dennis		

Also contained a small part of Rudheath Lordship (see note 11). A parochial chapelry of the parish of Great Budworth.

WOODCHURCH

1	Arrowe	6	Noctorum
2	Barnston	7	Oxton
3	Claughton cum Grange (small part, see note 16)	8	Pensby
		9	Prenton
4	Irby (greater part)	10	Thingwall
5	Landican	11	Woodchurch

For the origins of the parish see PNC IV 267.

WRENBURY CHAPELRY

1	Broomhall	5	Sound (part)
2	Chorley	6	Woodcott
3	Dodcott cum Wilkesley (part)	7	Wrenbury cum Frith
4	Newhall (part, see notes 6 and 13)		

A parochial chapelry of Acton. Burleydam chapel lay partly in Dodcott cum Wilkesley and partly in Newhall: "part of Dodcot cum Wilkesley called Smeaton Wood being nine houses, with some other parcells, and Burley-Dam" (Leycester).

WYBUNBURY

1	Basford	10	Hunsterson
2	Batherton	11	Lea
3	Blakenhall	12	Rope
4	Bridgemere	13	Shavington cum Gresty
5	Checkley cum Wrinehill (most of Wrinehill is in Staffs.)	14	Stapeley
		15	Walgherton
6	Chorlton	16	Weston
7	Doddington	17	Willaston (part)
8	Hatherton	18	Wybunbury
9	Hough		

The ancient parish was originally more extensive including the parishes of Audlem, Coppenhall and Wistaston, and, possibly Baddiley.

A LIST OF EXTRA-PAROCHIAL PLACES

Certain areas were not assimilated into the parochial system. The reasons are various and occasionally obscure, but chiefly they involve an association with religious houses or with the Crown. Where possible an explanation is given in the "Notes" or a reference to a source explaining the extra-parochial status of a particular place is appended.

Birkenhead	(See note 32).
Castle, Chester	
Cathedral precincts, Chester	
Grafton	(See note 36).
Great Stanney	(See note 3).
King's Marsh al. Overmarsh	(Orm II 752ff).
Little St. John, Chester	(See note 38).
Middleton Grange	(See note 30).
Overmarsh	(See King's Marsh).
Prior's Heys	(Orm II 307).
Rudheath	(See notes 4, 11 and 14, Orm III 168ff and PNC I 11-13).
Shotwick Park	(Orm II 571ff).
Spital Boughton, Chester	(Orm I 352). 1740 map places it with St. Oswald, but seems to have been included in Chester St John in 1778 (EDV 7/1/2). For the possibility of a chapel of Boughton distinct from the hospital see Gastrell 117.
Stanlow	(See note 2).
Threapwood	(part in Cheshire, part in Flints: PNC IV 61). A Chapel at Threapwood was consecrated by the Bishop of Chester in 1817
Willington	(granted to Stanlow Abbey, subsequently Whalley Abbey, Lancs.).

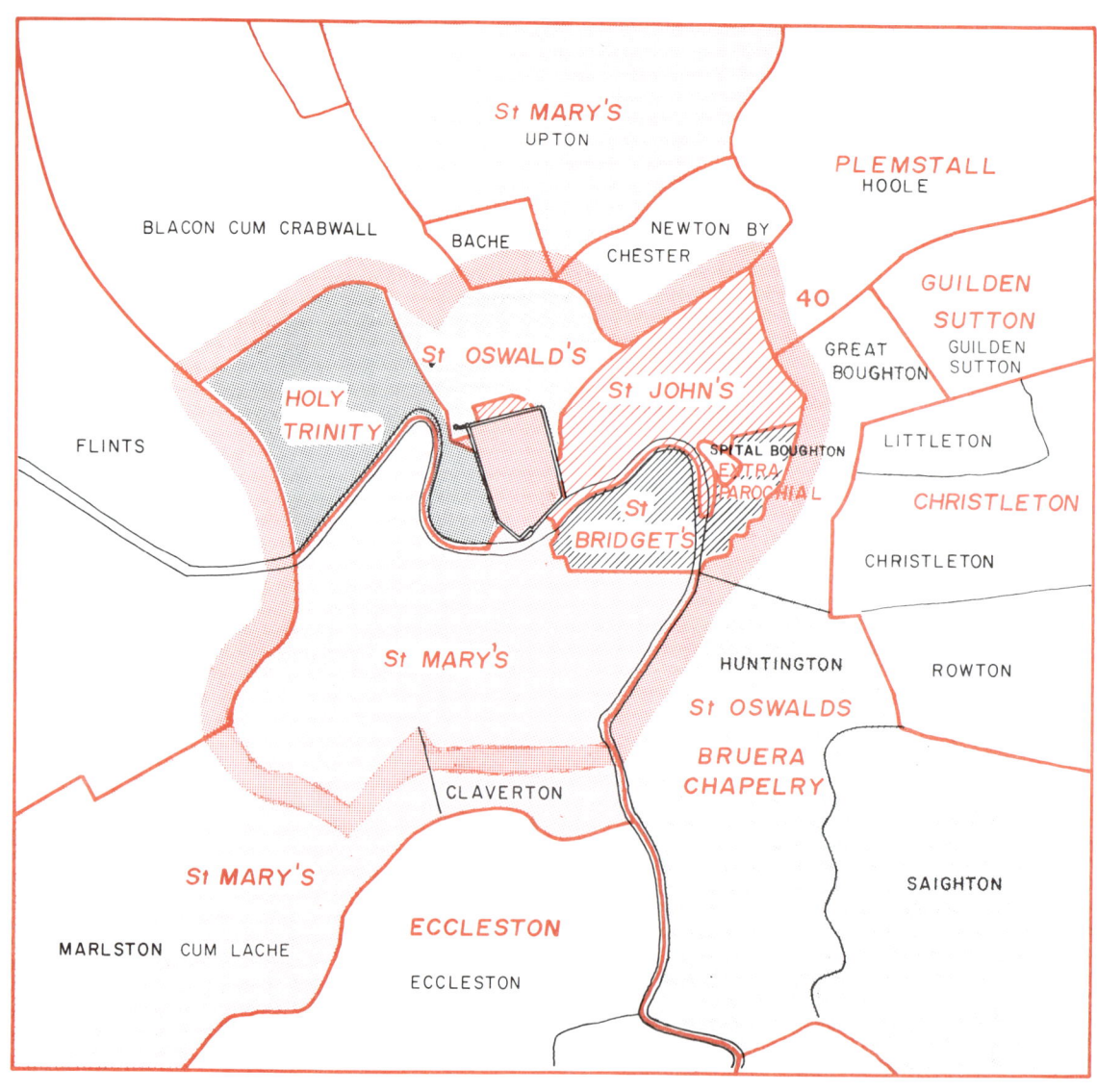

CHESTER PARISHES
(INNER AREA)

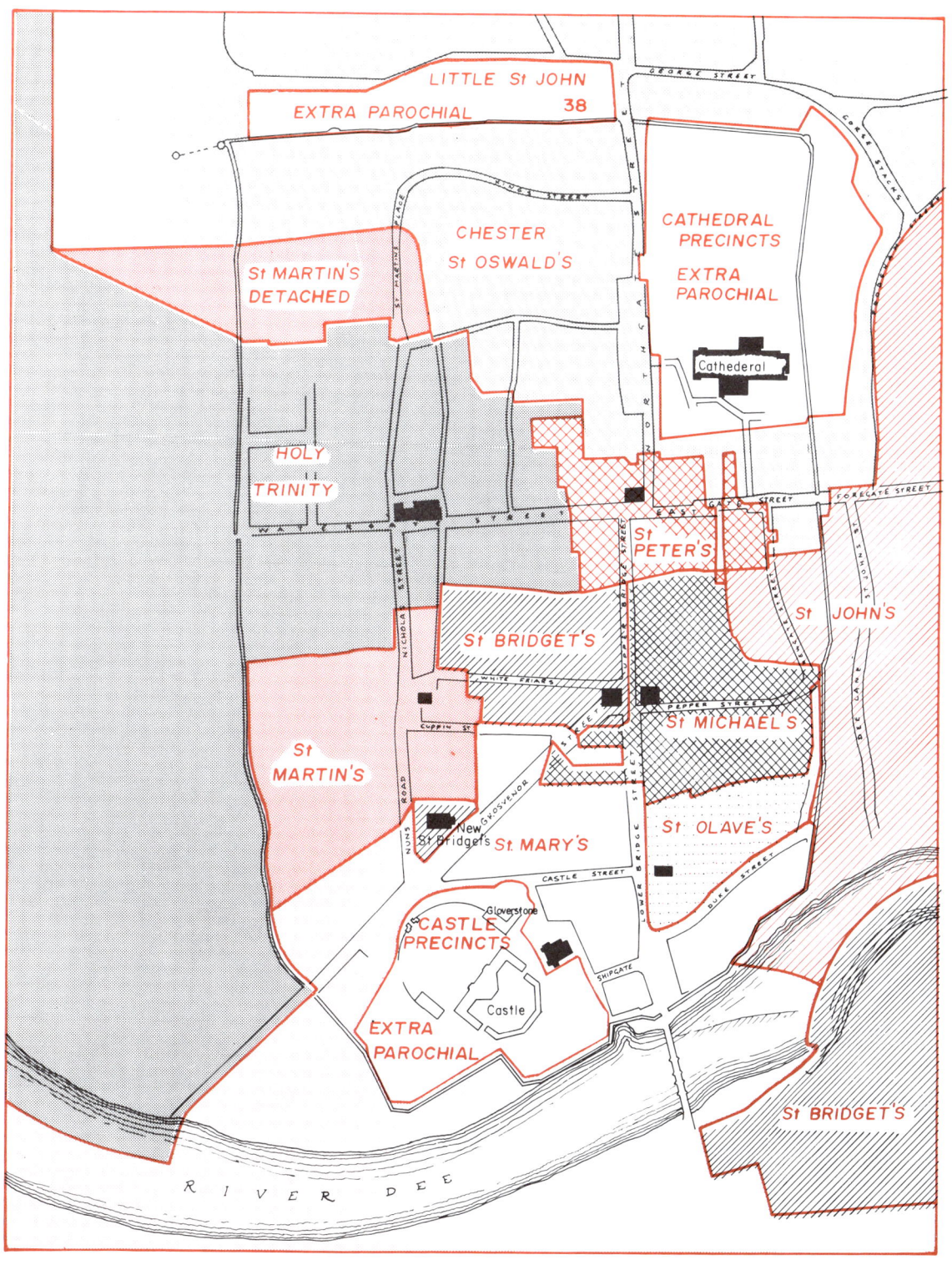

LITTLE St JOHN

EXTRA PAROCHIAL 38

GEORGE STREET

EXTRA PAROCHIAL

CHESTER St Oswald's

St MARTIN'S DETACHED

CATHEDRAL PRECINCTS

EXTRA PAROCHIAL

Cathederal

HOLY TRINITY

St PETER'S

FORGATE STREET

St JOHN'S

St BRIDGET'S

St MICHAEL'S

St MARTIN'S

New St Bridget's

St MARY'S

St OLAVE'S

CASTLE PRECINCTS

Gloverstone

Castle

EXTRA PAROCHIAL

St BRIDGET'S

R I V E R   D E E

NOTES
(Relating to both Maps and Lists)

1   The North-Westerly tip of Ince around "Holme House" was in Stoke parish.   (EDT 374/2).

2   Stanlow was a Cistercian monastery founded 1178 which removed to Whalley, Lancs in 1296 after an inundation by the sea. It was probably part of Great Stanney before this and remained extra-parochial after the dissolution of the cell maintained here by Whalley Abbey. (PNC IV 185). Leycester gives a classic description: "Stanlow-house formerly an Abbey is now in no Parish, nor hath it any Constable : but is a Priviledged place:"

3   The parish of Stoke contained the townships of Stoke, part of Whitby (see EDT 426/2) and the part of Ince that lay in Eddisbury Hundred (see note 1 above). Stanlow and Great Stanney, though extra-parochial seem later to have been included in Stoke parish, though anciently Eastham may have been the mother church. Great Stanney was extra-parochial as a result of being granted to Stanlow Abbey 1178. (PNC IV 182). Stoke was probably originally part of the parish of Chester St. Oswald which still had burial rights there in the late 13th cent (Orm II 389).

4   Earnshaw, a detached part of Rudheath Lordship in Sandbach parish.

5   Detached portions of Baddiley in Acton.

6   Detached portions of Newhall and Dodcott cum Wilkesley in Acton.

7   Detached portions of Whitegate parish.

8   A detached portion of Cheadle Moseley.

9   A detached portion of Marston.

10   Stublach, in Middlewich parish.

11   The extra-parochial status of Rudheath Lordship, despite parts being placed with various parishes for various purposes, is explained in PNC II 198.

12   A detached portion of Bradley.

13   The township of Newhall was partly in Audlem parish and partly in Wrenbury chapelry, with small detached parts in Acton parish proper (see note 6).

14   "No Town", a curious detached part of Rudheath in Twemlow township. (PNC II 230-1).

15   Hilbre Island and Little Eye form the township of Hilbre, a detached part of the parish of Chester St. Oswald. It may have been part of the parish of West Kirby before a cell of the abbey of St. Werburgh was founded there. (Orm II 501).

16   Part of the South-West corner of Claughton cum Grange adjoining the Oxton boundary was in Woodchurch parish. (EDT 47/2).

17   Blacon cum Crabwall, though reckoned as one township, is distinctly divided in that Crabwall lies in the parish of Chester St. Oswald, having been given to the abbey of St. Werburgh, while Blacon is in the parish of Chester, Holy Trinity. (Orm II 575-7).

18   A small southerly portion of Coole Pilate was in the parish of Audlem.

19   The apparent complication of the parishes of Whitegate and Over is explained by the presence of the abbey of Vale Royal. The church of the tenants of the abbey was made parochial at the dissolution of the abbey by statute 33 Henry VIII cap. 32, the parish being known as Whitegate or New Church. (Orm II 145 and PNC III 164).

20   Iddinshall was a detached part of the parish of Chester St. Oswald. (Orm II 305).

21 Bosden is the detached part of the township of Handforth cum Bosden in Cheadle parish. (Orm III 645).

22 The ancient parish of Cheadle comprises primarily the townships of Cheadle Bulkeley and Cheadle Moseley, so intermixed that it is impossible to depict on any small scale map. The townships may be distinguished by reference to the respective tithe maps. (EDT 90/2 and EDT 91/2). For an explanation of this complicated state of affairs see Orm III 621ff.

23 Bache, Great Boughton, Newton by Chester, Croughton, Wervin and a small part of Upton (EDT 407/2) all lay in the parish of Chester St. Oswald.

24 Claverton, Marlston cum Lache, Moston and the greater part of Upton all lay in the parish of Chester St. Mary.

25 Portions of Weaverham township comprising Hefferston Grange, Weaverham Wood and parts of Sandiway were in Whitegate parish (see note 19 above and PNC III 206-7).

26 A few fields of Norley lay in Crowton in Weaverham parish and, similarly, a few fields of Crowton lay in Norley (EDT 302/2).

27 Dutton lay in the parishes of Great Budworth and Runcorn (EDT 146/1 and 2). Poolsey al. Poosey, a detached chapelry (lost, but mentioned in EDV 7/1, 1778) of Runcorn parish, apparently lay near the Dutton/Bartington boundary in the township of Dutton. (PNC II 113). Poolsey chapel built c.1236 (Leycester). Its decline was attributed to "ye Neighbourhood resorting to the Domestic Chapel of Dutton" (Gastrell).

28 Stockton Heath is a hamlet in the township of Appleton, not a township as suggested in PNC II 145

29 Mutlow, the possible meeting place for the Domesday Hundred of Hamestan, in Marton township, was in the parish of Gawsworth. (PNC I 81).

30 Middleton Grange was an extra-parochial township and was not officially included in Aston by Sutton until 1843. (PNC II 161).

31 It has been conjectured that the ancient chapelry of Poynton included Woodford as well as Worth, (Orm III 684, but EDV 7/1/99, 1778 states categorically "Woodford is not in the Chapelry").

32 Birkenhead was an extra-parochial liberty created out of Claughton township to contain the demesne of Birkenhead Priory.

33 About 30 fields at the North-East corner of Baguley lay in Northenden parish. (EDT 34/2).

34 Leese is a township of Goostrey chapelry detached by Church Hulme Chapelry.

35 Sir Peter Leycester, in the mid 17th century, wrote of "an ancient free chapel at Warburton now usually taken for a parish church". (Orm I 566). It is shown as chapel of ease to Lymm (1740 Map).

36 Grafton was an extra-parochial liberty, which, though often regarded as a township of Tilston, did not officially become so until 1841. (PNC IV 61).

37 The township of Ashton on Mersey lay partly in Bowdon parish and partly in Ashton upon Mersey parish. The parts are completely intermixed and may be identified by reference to the respective tithe maps. (EDT 22/1 and EDT 23/1).

38 Little St. John, Chester, al. St. John of Jerusalem's Hospital, was stated in 1778 to consist of the Bluecoat Hospital, six alms houses and the Northgate Gaol. (EDV 7/1/3).

39 4 fields at the North-Eastern tip of the township of Backford were in Stoke parish. (EDT 31/2).

40 16 fields at the Southern tip of Hoole township lay in the parish of Chester St. John. (EDT 305/2).